traditional
irish
recipes

George L Thomson

The O'Brien Press

Copyright
©
1982
George L Thomson
All rights reserved

First published in Great Britain by
Canongate Publishing Limited · 17 Jeffrey Street · Edinburgh
ISBN · 0 · 86241 · 027 · 4

❖

First published in Ireland by
The O'Brien Press · 20 Victoria Road · Rathgar · Dublin
ISBN · 0 · 86278 · 110 · 8

❖

First published in the United States by
Pelican Publishing Company Inc.
1101 Monroe Street · Gretna · Louisiana · 70053
ISBN · 0 · 88289 · 339 · 4

❖

Library of Congress Cataloging in Publication Data
Thomson, George Lawrie.
Traditional Irish recipes.

Includes index.
1. Cookery, Irish. I. Title.
ISBN · 0 · 88289 · 339 · 4
TX717. 5. T48 1982   641.59415   82·16625

First published by The O'Brien Press Ltd.
Reprinted 1987, 1990.
Cover photograph: interior of an Irish cottage at
Bunratty Folk Park, courtesy Shannon Development.
Printed and bound by The Guernsey Press Co. Ltd.,
Guernsey, Channel Islands.

contents

anraith bhainbh
* GRUNT soup

1 dozen grunts · 1 lump butter · chopped chives · flou...
salt · pepper · hot water or milk·and·water

Clean and scale the grunts. Place in a pot and cover well
with hot water, cooking until tender. Lift out of the pot
and remove the skin and bones. Put the chives in the
stock and boil for a quarter of an hour. Add a good
lump of butter. When this is melted, mix in enough
blended flour to thicken the stock. Now add the fish and
boil for five minutes more. Serve with broken up boiled
potatoes.

* grunts are young perch

anraith preataí agus cainneann
Leek and potato soup

b potatoes · 1 lb leeks · 2 pints stock · 2 tblsp cream · 1 oz
utter · 1 cup croutons · 1 stick white celery · salt · pepper

Dice the potatoes, and chop up the leeks and celery. Melt the
butter in a pan, add the vegetables and toss thoroughly.
Replace the lid and cook lightly for at least five minutes
without sizzling. Now add the stock, [meat or chicken].
Half milk and water will serve if you have no stock. Season
to taste and simmer for about an hour. Fry a cupful of
croutons and whip the cream. Place croutons in a soup
tureen and pour in the soup. Stir in the whipped cream
and serve immediately.

anraith neantóg
nettle pottage

2 pints stock · 2 oz rough oatmeal · 2 oz butter · 1 pint of
nettle tops

❖

Finely chop the nettle tops. Melt the butter and fry the oatmeal
until crisp and brown. [Coarse oatmeal provides more
texture than medium or fine.] Add the stock, which
may be vegetable, meat or milk; during hard times, water
had to suffice. Bring to the boil, add the chopped nettle
tops, and boil a further five or ten minutes.

anraith gaelach
irish broth

3 pints stock · 3 pints nettle tops · 3 oz fine oatmeal · 2 oz
butter · 2 onions · 1 large leek · 1 egg yolk · ¼ pint cream ·
grated nutmeg · salt · pepper

Finely chop the onions and sauté in hot butter. Add the fine
oatmeal, the finely chopped nettles and leek, the stock and
the seasonings, and cook slowly for about an hour. Beat
the yolk of egg and cream together and carefully stir into
the soup. Check seasoning, reheat, but do not bring to boil.

4

anraith eascainne
eel soup

1 dozen small eels · ½ lb spinach · ½ lb lettuce · 2 leeks · 2 butter · 3 egg yolks · 1 onion · ¼ pint cream · 3 pints fish stock [or water] · 3 oz crackers · chopped fennel and dill salt · pepper

❖

Skin the eels and cut into small pieces. Fry the sliced onion and leeks lightly, add the eels and fry for five minutes more. Add the stock and bring to the boil. Simmer until eels are fully cooked, then remove and bone. Cut into cubes. Strain the stock, and return the eels, along with the chopped lettuce and spinach. Simmer very gently for eight minutes, then thicken the soup with crumbled and sieved crackers, seasoning to taste. Beat the egg yolks and cream together, and stir into the soup. Before serving, sprinkle with the chopped fennel and dill.

anraith preataí
potato soup

ashers streaky bacon · 2 lbs potatoes · 2 oz butter · 1½ pts
lk · 1½ pts stock · 1 cup cream · 2 onions · pepper · salt ·
chopped parsley

❖

eel and slice the onions, and fry gently in the melted butter,
without allowing them to brown. Add the peeled and
sliced potatoes, and pour over the milk and stock, seasoned
to taste. Cover and simmer gently for one hour. Sieve,
add the cream and re-heat, but do not allow to boil. The
streaky bacon should be fried crisp, then broken up finely
with a fork. Use this as a garnish on top of the soup, along
with the chopped parsley, or chopped chives.

anraith ruacáin
cockle soup

2 quarts cockles · 2 onions · 1 pint milk · 2 sticks celer
2 tblsp chopped parsley · 1½ oz butter · 1½ oz flour · peppe
2 pints cockle stock · 1 cup of cream · a few cloves · sa

Wash the cockles very thoroughly to remove all sand. Put in
a pot with two pints of sea water [or salted water] and bring
to the boil. When the shells open, remove from the heat, discar
the shells and keep the cockles in a warm bowl. Finely chop
one onion, fry in the butter and add the chopped parsley and
celery. Add the strained stock, the milk, and a whole onion
stuck with a few cloves. Bring to the boil and simmer twenty
minutes, then thicken with the flour mixed in a little milk.
Add the cockles and re-heat for a few minutes. Serve with
a spoonful of cream on each plateful.

brachan rolchep
brotchan roltchep

pints milk [or stock] · 6 leeks · 1 oz butter · 2 tblsp medium
oatmeal · 1 tblsp chopped parsley · salt · pepper

Use good sized leeks. Wash and cut up into inch long pieces,
using the green leaves as well as the stalks. Put the milk
or stock in a pan with the butter, and heat. when it
boils, add the oatmeal, stirring to prevent lumping. After
a few minutes, add the chopped leeks and seasoning.
Replace lid and simmer gently about fortyfive minutes,
then add the parsley and cook a few minutes more.
In the past, when leeks were not available, nettles were used
instead. Here one would substitute a cupful of chopped
young nettle tops for each leek. A little cream is a
delicious addition to this dish.

Trosc bacálta na Gaillimhe
Baked Galway codlin

2 lbs codling · 3 dozen cockles · 12 potatoes · 8 small oni
1 lemon · 2 oz butter · 1 tblsp chopped parsley · thyme · sa
pepper

♣

Clean and rinse the cockles and place in a saucepan with a
little water. Cover and cook over a moderate heat, shaking
occasionally. Remove from shells and put into a greased
baking tin with the fish. Season with salt, pepper and
chopped thyme. Arrange the onions and parboiled potatoes
round the fish, and pour over the cockle juice. Melt the
butter and pour over all. Bake in a hot oven, 450°F, for
fifteen to twenty minutes. Serve garnished with chopped
parsley and slices of lemon.

9

cloichean bhaile atha cliath
dublin bay prawns

2 lbs prawns · 3 oz butter · 1 lemon [juice] · salt · pepper

♣

Clean, and steam the prawns for fifteen to twenty minutes.
Allow to cool, then shell them. Melt the butter in a pan,
add the prawns and mix thoroughly. Season to taste,
then add the lemon juice and mix all together. The
butter should become a delicate pink colour. Garnish with
sprigs of parsley.

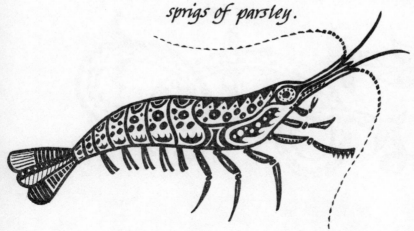

eascain stobhach
steuued eels

4 lbs eels · 1 tblsp chopped parsley · 1 tblsp chopped chive
white sauce · salt · pepper

First parboil the eels so that they can be skinned more easily.
Cut up the skinned eels into three or four inch lengths. Put
in a saucepan, cover with cold water and bring to the boil.
Allow to boil a few minutes, then drain and dry. Make a
white sauce and add to it the chopped chives and the eels.
Stew for three quarters of an hour, add the chopped parsley,
and serve hot.

11

OISRE FRIOCHTA
FRIED OYSTERS

4 dozen oysters · 4 eggs · 8 oz flour · butter · salt · pepper

❖

beat the eggs and add the salt, pepper and flour, along with the liquor from the oysters, to make a smooth batter. Open the oysters and beard them. Dip the oysters in the batter and fry golden brown in boiling clarified butter. Do not overcook. Serve with wedges of lemon and garnish with sprigs of parsley.

breac griosetha
grilled trout

1 1½ lb trout · 2 oz butter · 1 lemon · 8 shallots · 1 tblsp
parsley · 1 tblsp chives · basil · salt · pepper

❧

Clean and bone the trout. Finely chop the parsley, chives, basil
and shallots, then mix with the butter, adding lemon juice,
grated lemon rind, and salt and pepper to taste. Use this
mixture to stuff the trout. Wrap it in greaseproof paper
and lay on a well buttered dish. Bake in the oven at 350°F.
for twenty minutes or so.

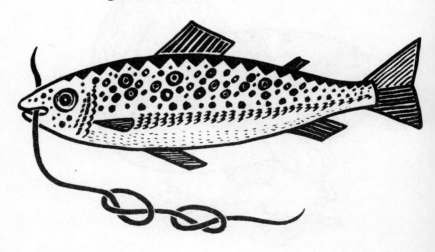

13

bradan scallta
poached salmon

1 salmon · 1 oz butter · 1 onion · sprigs of parsley · 1 bay leaf · salt · pepper

♣

Clean and wash the salmon. Put the other ingredients in a fish kettle with enough water [or water and milk] to cover the fish. Boil for two minutes, then simmer, allowing five minutes per pound plus five minutes. Drain and place on a large dish, on a bed of Colcannon [which see]. Strain the liquid in which the salmon was poached, and with it make a rich white sauce, which is served with the fish. Garnish with sprigs of parsley.

bealain
willocks

These are periwinkles or winkles [buckies in Scotland],
small shellfish with a coiled snail-like shell

Traditionally these are boiled in sea water for ten minutes then
"winkled" out of their shells with a pin, and eaten either plain
or dipped in fine oatmeal. (For a more sophisticated dish,
after boiling and taking out of their shells, wash well to remove
any sand, and place in a saucepan with salt and pepper.
Boil a further twenty minutes, simmer until tender, and strain.
In one pint of milk, boil ¼ lb of carragheen moss, and simmer
until it thickens. Strain into the saucepan and simmer ten
more minutes before serving.

píog an Ruacáin
cocklety pie

2 quarts cockles · 2 onions · 1 pint milk · 2 sticks celery ·
2 tblsp chopped parsley · 1½ oz butter · 1½ oz flour · pepper ·
salt

❖

Wash the cockles very thoroughly to remove all sand. Put in a
pot with a pint of sea water [or salted water] and bring to
the boil. When the shells open, remove from the heat, discard
the shells and keep the cockles in a warm bowl. Finely chop
one onion, fry in the butter and add the chopped parsley and
celery. Add the strained stock, the milk, and a whole onion
stuck with a few cloves. Bring to the boil and simmer twenty
minutes, then thicken with the flour mixed in a little milk.
Boil ten more minutes, then strain over the cockles. Cover with
a pastry crust and bake at 350°F. for thirty minutes or so.

scadaín saíllte
pickled herring

8 herrings · 1 large onion · cloves · peppercorns · 2 bay leave
salt · pepper · vinegar

Clean and bone the herrings, removing heads and tails. Arrange
in a piedish and add the thinly sliced onion, a few cloves,
peppercorns and bay leaves, and a sprinkle of salt. Barely
cover with equal quantities of vinegar and water. Bake for
about one hour in a slow oven, then allow to cool in the liquor.
May be served hot with floury potatoes, or cold with a salad.
Try mackerel, also delicious when prepared in the same way.

eochraí truisc
cod's roe ramekins

1b boiled cod roe · 4 oz breadcrumbs · 1 egg · 1 cup milk ·
2 tsp chopped parsley · pepper and salt

❧

Chop up and mash the cod roe, and mix with the parsley, salt
and pepper, and the breadcrumbs. Beat the egg yolk, add
the milk and pour over the mixture. Leave for ten minutes
or so until the breadcrumbs are soaked through. Stiffly
beat the egg white and fold into the mixture. Grease six
ramekins and spoon in until nearly filled. Bake in a
hot oven, 400°F., for around fifteen minutes until risen
firm and golden brown.

aturnae bhaile atha cliath
dublin lawyer

1 large lobster · 4 oz butter · 4 tblsp cream · salt · peppe
4 tblsp Irish whiskey

❖

Cut the lobster in two lengthwise and remove the meat, including the claws, and keeping the shells. Melt the butter, not overheating, and put in the lobster meat, cut into large pieces. Salt and pepper. Warm the whiskey, pour over and set alight. Add the cream and mix with the juices in the pan. Heat well, but do not allow to boil. Serve hot, arranged in the half shells.

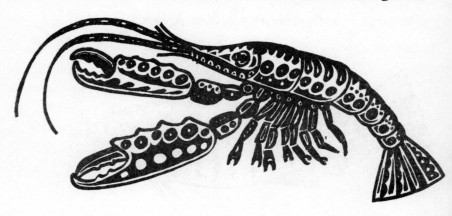

muirín scallops

zen scallops · 1 oz flour · 1 oz butter · chopped parsley · salt · pepper · lemon juice

Wash the scallops well, open and remove the beards and black parts. Wash in cold water. Place in a saucepan, cover with warm water. Simmer gently for ten minutes, then remove from the water. Mix flour and butter together over low heat to make a roux, carefully adding the liquid from the scallops to prevent lumps, and continue cooking until it thickens. Place the scallops on a hot dish. Season the sauce to taste, add a dessertspoonful of lemon juice and pour over the scallops. Garnish with chopped parsley.

cadog uachta rui
creamed haddock

1 lb haddock fillets · 4 oz butter · ¼ pint cream · ¼ pin
1 tsp mustard · salt · pepper · flour

Mix some salt and pepper into the flour and roll the fillets
in it to cover. Melt the butter and dip the fillets in it, then
lay them in a pan. Add any surplus butter with the milk an.
cream, then heat gently to bubbling point. Reduce heat an.
simmer gently until the fish is cooked, then remove and keep
hot on a serving dish. To the remaining liquid, add a good
spoonful of made up mustard, mix well, and reduce over heat
until slightly thickened. Pour this sauce over the fish.
Serve decorated with sprigs of parsley. This recipe can be
used for ANY white fish - cod, plaice etc.

sól gaelach
irish sole

1 large sole · mushroom stuffing · salt · pepper · lemon juice or vinegar

(For mushroom stuffing: 4 oz mushrooms · 3 oz breadcrumbs · 1 oz margarine · 2 egg yolks · 1 tsp chopped parsley · juice of ½ lemon · salt · pepper

Fillet and skin the sole. Wash carefully and dry, then season well, rubbing in salt, pepper and lemon juice. Spread with the mushroom stuffing and fold over. (Place on a greased baking tin and round it pour a little fish stock. Or dot the fish with knobs of butter. Cover with greased paper and bake at 350°F. until tender. Serve hot, covered with cheese sauce, garnished with parsley, grated cheese and slices of mushroom.
Stuffing: (Finely chop the mushrooms and cook gently in the melted margarine. Add the breadcrumbs, lemon juice, parsley, salt and pepper and mix thoroughly, binding all together with the lightly beaten egg yolks.

gliomach bacálta
baked lobster

2 two-pound lobsters · 2 medium onions · 4 mushrooms · 2 shallots · ½ tsp chopped tarragon · 2 oz flour · 3 oz butter · ¼ tsp dry mustard · milk · sherry

boil the lobsters for twenty minutes in boiling salted water. Split them lengthwise. Remove the meat from tail and claws and cut in one inch pieces, saving the coral. Sauté the chopped mushrooms, onions and shallots in the butter until golden, then add the flour and mustard and mix to a smooth paste. Add three cups of hot milk, stir until it thickens, and add the lobster meat and coral and sherry to taste. Heat piping hot and pour on to a heated dish. Decorate with creamed potatoes piped round, and garnish with lobster claws and sprigs of parsley.

mairteoil shaillte agus cabáiste
corned beef & cabbage

bs corned beef · 1 large cabbage · 1 large carrot · bunch of
yme and parsley · 1 tsp dry mustard · cloves · salt · pepper

lace the corned beef in a large saucepan. Add the carrot, sliced;
the whole onions, one stuck with a few cloves; the mustard
and herbs. Bring to the boil and skim, then cover and
simmer slowly for fortyfive minutes.* Now add the cabbage,
cleaned and cut in quarters. Cook for two hours, then serve
the meat surrounded by cabbage. The saved stock may
be used as a soup base, and is very good with dried peas,
split, yellow or green.

* Season.

COINÍN RÓSTA
ROAST RABBIT

1 rabbit · 2 medium onions · 2 oz butter · 4 rashers bac
1 tblsp flour · 1 dsstsp chopped parsley · ½ pint scalded
pepper

✤

Clean and cut up the rabbit into convenient sized pieces and soak
in vinegar and water. Dry the joints well, then dredge in
flour well seasoned with pepper. Brown nicely in the heated
butter. Place in a casserole with the chopped bacon, onions
and parsley. Pour the milk over all, cover, and bake for
one hour at 375°F. This should be served with floury
boiled potatoes and parsley sauce.

gé ꝼheil mhichil
michaelmas goose

1b goose · goose giblets · Stuffing – 1½ lbs boiled potatoes.
medium onion · ½ cup salt bacon · 1 goose liver · 1 tblsp
opped parsley · 1 tsp chopped sage · salt and pepper

Mash the potatoes, dice the onion and bacon, chop the liver,
add the chopped parsley and sage, season thoroughly with
salt and pepper, and mix all together. Use this to stuff
the bird. Make a stock with the goose giblets, and add a
cupful of this to the roasting pan in which you put the
goose. Cover with foil and roast in a hot oven, 400° F. for
about three hours.

26

TOIR CEOIL
pig's head brawn

½ pig's head · 2 onions · 1 bunch herbs · a few cloves · pepp
salt · saltpetre

❧

First wash the head thoroughly in warm water, then rub it all over
with a mixture of salt and saltpetre. Leave for three days,
then place in a saucepan and cover with cold water. Bring to
boil and simmer until the meat will leave the bones. Take out
the head, remove the bones and return them to the stock with
the quartered onions, herbs and cloves. Boil again for about
thirty minutes, then strain into a basin. In the meantime,
chop the meat small and place in a mould, seasoned to taste.
Pour over it enough stock to moisten without making it sodden.
Cover and leave to cool and set, when it is ready to serve

27

Dresín Drisheen

b mutton suet · 1 quart milk · 1 quart sheep's blood · 2 cups
eadcrumbs · 1 pint water · ¼ tsp white pepper · 1 dsstsp salt ·
pinch of tansy and thyme

Finely chop the mutton suet. Strain the blood into a bowl, and
add all the other ingredients, mixing thoroughly. Allow to
stand a short time. Transfer the mixture into a well
greased ovenproof dish, and cover with greased paper, securely
tied. Steam for about fifty minutes, or bake in a fairly
moderate oven, 300°F, for approximately the same time.
When ready, cut into squares and put on a hot dish. Garnish
with a small sprig of parsley on each square, with grilled
slices of tomato placed round the edge.

pióg mhuiceola ✤
pork ciste

6 pork chops· 3 pork kidneys· [or, ½ lb pig liver]· 1 large
carrot· 2 medium onions· 1 tblsp chopped parsley· ½ tb
chopped thyme· 1 bay leaf· salt· pepper· 1 pint stock app
(Pastry for the ciste: 8 oz flour· 4 oz grated suet· ½ cup sultar
½ cup milk· 1 tsp baking powder· ½ tsp salt

♣

Place the chops bone end up round the inside of a saucepan, after
removing surplus fat. In the centre put chopped liver or kidney,
sliced carrot & onions and herbs; season well and barely cover
with stock. Replace lid tightly. Simmer 30 minutes. To make
the ciste, mix the ingredients to a stiff dough. Roll on a
floured board to fit the saucepan, and press down on the stew.
Make sure there is enough space left for rising, replace lid
and cook on gentle heat for one to one and a half hours.
If preferred, may be cooked in the oven; 350°F., same time.

✤ Lamb Ciste- Pióg Uaineola – may be made in exactly the
same way, using lamb chops, kidneys and liver, but missing
out the sultanas used in the pork ciste.

COININ RÓSTAITHE
POT ROAST RABBIT

2 young rabbits · ½ lb fat bacon · ½ pint milk · pepper · salt · 1½ tsp salt in 1½ pts water

Cut up the rabbits into joints, using the best parts, and make stock with the rest. Use the 1½ pints of salt water to soak the joints for three hours, then remove and dry. The bacon should be quite thickly sliced, and each slice should be cut in two before frying – slowly, to extract the fat. Then remove on to a plate. Mix the pepper and salt with a tablespoon of flour and toss the rabbit joints in this. Fry quickly until nicely browned. Put in a heavy stew pan with the bacon on top, replace the lid, and cook very gently for 1–1½ hours, turning the meat occasionally to ensure even cooking. When tender, add the milk and continue cooking for another 30 minutes.

smig mhuiceoile
chine of bacon

1 chine of bacon · 12 peppercorns · 1 tblsp brown sugar · 1 bay leaf · 2 blackcurrant leaves · 1 tblsp chives · cloves · 1 tsp sage · 1 tsp marjoram · 1 tsp rosemary · 1 tsp thyme · ½ tsp black pepper

The bacon should be soaked overnight. Next day, carefully scrape the rind, rinse well and dry. Finely chop the herbs, including the blackcurrant leaves, and add the black pepper. Mix all together. Now make a series of deep cuts in the bacon and stuff with the herb mixture. The bacon should now be tied in a piece of fine muslin to retain this. Put into a pan of cold water the sugar, peppercorns, bayleaf and two cloves, add the bacon and bring to the boil. Reduce the heat and simmer very slowly, allowing twentyfive minutes to the pound. Then remove from the pan and drain. Detach the muslin. Take off the rind. To finish, stud all over with cloves, or dredge with golden brown bread crumbs.

PRÓG CHOLUIR
pigeon pie

pigeons · ½ lb stewing steak · 1 hardboiled egg · ½ lb flaky pastry · ½ lb bacon · 1 dsstsp flour · 1 tsp salt · 1 tsp chopped parsley · stock · ½ tsp salt · egg or milk to glaze

Pluck and clean the pigeons and cut off the feet. Cut each bird in four pieces. Season the flour, dip each piece in it and arrange in a piedish. Cut up the steak into small pieces and add. Do the same with the bacon, add the hardboiled egg and the parsley and sufficient stock to half fill the dish. Cover with the pastry, decorate, and glaze with egg or milk. Bake in a hot oven, 450°F., to start with, then lower the temperature and cook for one and a half hours, or until the pigeons are tender. When the pie is finally cooked, fill it up with stock.

trosc bhaile atha cliath

dublin coddle

2 lbs potatoes · 8 pork sausages · 8 ham or bacon slices · 4 large onions · 4 tblsp chopped parsley · 1 qut boiling water salt · pepper

❦

The ¼" thick ham slices should be cut into large chunks. Boil for 5 minutes with the sausages. Drain, keeping the stock, and put in a large saucepan with the peeled and sliced potatoes, finely sliced onions and chopped parsley. Season, and barely cover with stock. Cover with greaseproof paper, replace the lid and simmer gently for about an hour or until cooked, but do not allow to become soft and mushy. If preferred, cook in a casserole in the oven, 200°F. Serve hot, with the vegetables on top. Traditionally accompanied by fresh soda bread and stout.

teanga spíosraithe
spiced tongue

1 salted ox or calf tongue · 1 large onion · cloves · sprig of thyme · sprig of parsley · 1 tblsp aspic jelly powder · pepper

When trimming off the gristly part at the root of the tongue, leave enough to make sure the stock will jelly. Soak overnight in cold water. Stick the onion with four or five cloves, and place in a pot with the tongue and other ingredients. Cover with cold water and simmer four hours or until the meat is tender. To skin the tongue more easily, remove from the stock and plunge in ice-cold water. If to be served cold, after skinning and trimming, coil it in a circle in a suitable basin. Strain about two cupfuls of stock, add the aspic powder, boil till dissolved and pour over the tongue. When cool put a weighted plate on top and leave overnight. Cut into thick slices. Serve hot or cold with this accompanying sauce. See page 35 for ingredients.

Ingredients for the sauce

1 cup tongue stock · 1 cup red wine or 1 cup port · ½ cup
red currant jelly · 1 lemon · 1 orange · 2 tblsp tarragon
vinegar · 1 tblsp horse radish, freshly grated · 1 tsp
dry mustard powder

❧

Finely grate the lemon and the orange, squeeze the juice, and
put together with all the other ingredients in a suitable pan.
Boil for about thirty minutes, by which time the sauce
should be reduced and thickened in texture.   The thick
slices of tongue, when serving hot, should be thoroughly
heated in the sauce.

mairteoil spiosraithe
spiced beef

6 lb beef joint · 4 medium onions · 3 carrots · ½ pint stout ·
1 stick celery · 3 whole cloves · 1 tsp ground cloves · 1 tsp allspice
(To spice a 6 lb joint : 1 lb rock salt · 6 blades mace · 3 bay leaves ·
1 clove garlic · 1 tsp allspice · 1 tsp peppercorns · 1 tsp cloves · 2 heaped
tblsp brown sugar · 2 heaped tblsp saltpetre

Pound the garlic and bay leaves into a mixture of the ingredients for
spicing. Rub this all over the joint in a large dish. Turn daily
for a week, covering with the spices from the dish. Wash & tie.
Slice three of the onions and the carrots, also the celery, and place
with the other ingredients in a large saucepan, with the already
spiced joint on top. Cover with cold water, bring slowly to the
boil, and skim. Simmer gently for four hours, adding the
half pint of stout at the end of three hours.
If serving cold, place on a large plate, with another weighted
plate on top, and leave overnight.

struisin gaelach
irish stew

3 lb lean neck of lamb chops · 2 lb potatoes · 1 lb onions ·
3/4 pint water · sprig of parsley · sprig of thyme · pepper ·
salt

Cut the chops into largish chunks, but trim away surplus fat
and gristle. Bones may be left in. Peel the potatoes. Thinly
slice one third, leaving the rest whole unless they are large, when
they may be cut to a more convenient size. Place the sliced
potatoes in a pan, then a layer of the sliced onions, then the meat.
Now add the remaining onions with the chopped parsley and thyme.
Finish off the top with the whole potatoes. Add the water and
season to taste. Cover tightly, and place in the oven at 325°F
for 2 - 2½ hours. If preferred, the stew may be cooked in a
saucepan on top of the stove. Simmer gently, and check to see it
does not become too dry.

ჩiarrfhia gaelach
irish hare

hare · 1 pint stock · 3 oz flour · ¾ lb beef dripping · one
carrot · 1 large onion · 1 small turnip · salt · pepper

int the hare, wash and dry it. (Dice the turnip, carrot and
onion and fry in a stewpan. Add the joints of hare and
cook very slowly with the lid on for thirty minutes. Mix
the flour with a little of the stock and stir into the stewpan.
Add the remaining stock and simmer for two more hours.
Serve with redcurrant jelly and forcemeat balls.

CRUIBINI
CRUBEENS

1 dozen pig's trotters · 1 carrot · 1 onion · 1 bay leaf
small bunch thyme & parsley · salt · pepper

✤

Take a large saucepan and in it place the pig's feet, one
large carrot and one large onion cut up roughly, the bay
leaf, thyme and parsley, and add sufficient water to
cover completely.   Season to taste with salt and pepper.
Crubeens can be served hot or cold.   When cold, they
will be in a savoury jelly.   Soda bread and a glass
of stout are traditional accompaniments to this dish.

putoga agus onniun
tripe and onions

1 lb tripe · 1 lb onions · 1 pint milk · 2 slices lean ham, or bacon · 2 tblsp chopped parsley · 2 tblsp cornflour · breadcrumbs · salt · pepper

✤

The tripe should be boiled several times, starting with cold water, then cut up into pieces about two inches square. Roughly chop up the ham or bacon. Peel and slice the onions. Place these ingredients in a pan with the milk, and season to taste. Cover, and simmer gently for two hours. If preferred, it may be cooked in a slow oven instead. Now mix the cornflour in a tablespoon of cold water, stir it in, and again bring to the boil, remembering to keep stirring meanwhile. Five minutes before serving, add the chopped parsley. sprinkle breadcrumbs on top, then brown carefully under the grill.

brúitín
champ

8 potatoes · 6 scallions · 4 oz butter · ⅓ pint milk · pepper
salt

❖

Peel and boil the potatoes. Drain and mash. Chop the scallions,
and cook in the milk. Remove the scallions, add to
the mashed potatoes with pepper and salt, and beat well
together, adding just enough milk to make it creamy
smooth. Place in a deep, warmed dish, and make a well
in the centre to receive the hot melted butter. Each
spoonful is dipped in the butter when serving. In olden
days, chopped fresh young nettle tops would be used in
place of the scallions.

41

saleid samhaidh
sorrel salad

1 lb sorrel leaves · 8 pickled mushrooms · lemon juice · oil

Take one pound of fresh young sorrel leaves, remove the stalks and shred finely. Mix in the mushrooms. Make up a salad dressing with oil and lemon juice, and mix with the mushrooms and sorrel. Garnish each portion of salad with a small mushroom.

42

onniun saillte
pickled onions

small onions· vinegar· 2 tsp allspice and 2 tsp whole
black peppercorns for each 2 pints of vinegar

Peel the desired quantity of small onions and pack into suitable
jars. Boil the vinegar with the spice and peppercorns
and pour over the onions, being careful to cover them.
Cover tightly and store in a dry cupboard. If the vinegar
is used cold, the pickles will be ready for use in about
two weeks. If hot vinegar is used, they will be ready sooner.

43

cál ceannann
colcannon

8 potatoes · 1 small cabbage · ⅓ pint milk · 1 oz butter ·
scallions · parsley · salt · pepper

Peel, boil and mash the potatoes. Finely chop the scallions, add
to the potatoes, pour on boiling milk and beat until fluffy.
Cook the cabbage, chop up finely and pour on the melted
butter. Add to the potatoes with chopped parsley, salt and
pepper, and beat well, keeping all hot over a low heat
meanwhile.   Melted butter may be added to individual
servings if desired. Kale can be substituted for cabbage in
season, and leeks for scallions. Leftovers may be fried in
bacon fat until crisp and browned on both sides.

meacan bán taortha
toasted parsnips

3 parsnips · 4 oz butter · salt and pepper · castor sugar

Wash and clean the parsnips, cut across in short pieces, about one inch. Add seasoning to water, and boil for around half an hour. Drain and dry. Heat the butter in the frying pan and toss the parsnips in it. Sprinkle with sugar and brown nicely under grill.

onniun bhacálta
baked onions

4 large onions · salt · pepper

Place the onions, unpeeled, in a baking tin with an inch or less depth of cold water. Bake in the oven for one and a half to two hours at 250° - 275°F. They are ready when soft to the touch. Peel down the skins and cut off at the root. Serve with salt and pepper and a pat of butter. This is traditionally eaten along with Pratie Oaten.

Dulease
Dulse

dulse · butter · milk · pepper

Dulse is sold in dried form. To prepare, soak for three hours in cold water. Remove and allow to drain, then simmer for three hours in hot milk to which has been added a knob of butter and a seasoning of pepper. Dulse is a reddish brown seaweed which can be found all round the coast of Ireland. Local names for it are dillisk or dillesk. Its scientific name is Rhodymenia Palmata.

Gleabhacán
sloke

sloke · butter · cream · lemon juice

Place the sloke in a pan, cover with water and bring to the boil. Simmer for four to five hours. Drain well. Serve with a knob of butter and a drop of cream, and finish with a squeeze of lemon juice. It is a suitable vegetable to accompany most main courses. Like dulse, it is found round all the coast of Ireland. It is also called sea spinach, and in England and Wales, laver. The Latin names are Porphyra – purple laver, and Ulva – green laver.

glothach an charraigí
carragheen jelly

¼ oz carragheen · 1 pint milk · 1 dsstsp sugar · lemon rind
salt

♣

Cover the dried carragheen moss with cold water and leave
to soak for ten to fifteen minutes. Remove any discoloured
parts. Place in a saucepan with the milk, lemon rind
and salt. Bring to the boil and simmer until it coats the
back of a wooden spoon. Add the sugar and stir until
dissolved. Strain into a wet mould and leave in a cool
place to set. Turn out on a glass dish and serve with
fresh or stewed fruit.

ciste bheath-uisce gaelach
irish whiskey cake

½ glass Irish whisky · ⅔ glass sherry · ½ pint milk ·
6 square sponge cakes · ½ pint whipped cream · almonds ·
½ cup jam · 2 eggs

Slice squares of sponge cake and sandwich together with jam.
Put in a glass dish and moisten with the whiskey and
sherry; more than the given quantities may be used,
according to taste! Cover over all with custard made
from the eggs, milk and sugar, but cool before pouring.
Decorate with whipped cream and almonds.

bairin breac
barm brack

1 lb flour · 8 oz sultanas · 8 oz currants · 4 oz mixed peel
2 oz butter · 2 oz brown sugar · 2 eggs · ½ oz yeast · ½ pt m
¼ tsp nutmeg · salt

❧

All the ingredients must be at blood heat. Sift together the flour, nutmeg and salt, and rub in the butter. Cream the yeast with a teaspoon of sugar in a little of the tepid milk. Mix the remaining sugar with the flour. Add the milk to the yeast and beaten eggs, keeping aside a little of the egg to glaze the bread, if required. Beat the liquid into the dry ingredients until the batter is stiff but elastic, then fold in the dried fruit and peel. Turn into a buttered 8" cake tin, cover with a cloth and leave to rise in a warm place for one hour. Bake in the oven at 400°F. for one hour. Use egg to glaze the top, and return to oven for four or five minutes. An alternative glaze can be made with two tablespoons of boiling water with one tablespoon of sugar dissolved in it.

Turn out to cool on a wire tray.

51

bruitin ullach
pratie apple

oz potatoes · 4 oz flour · 3 cooking apples · sugar · salt ·
butter · honey · ½ tsp baking powder

Boil and mash the potatoes, add the flour and salt, and make
a dough. Roll out into a circle and cut in quarters.
Slice the apples and place on two of the triangles. Cover
with the other two and seal down the edges. Cook on the
griddle. When cooked cut a hole in the top of each and
put in a generous helping of sugar and honey with a
little butter. Allow all this to melt, and serve very hot.

52

arán sóid
soda bread

1 lb flour · ½ tsp salt · ½ tsp bread soda · ½ pint butterm

Add the salt and soda to the flour and sieve into a bowl.
Make a well in the middle and add the buttermilk [or
sour or fresh milk.] Stir into a soft dough, using a
wooden spoon. Knead lightly with floury hands. Turn
out on to a floured board. Flatten with the palm of the
hand into a circle about 1½ inches thick. With a floured
knife, mark a cross on the top, so it will break into four
pieces when cooked. Bake in the oven at 400°F. for
about forty minutes.

builbhin torthaí giosta
yeasty fruit loaf

20 oz plain flour · 5 oz raisins · 4 oz butter · 4 oz sugar · 2 oz yeast · 2 eggs · 2 tblsp mashed potatoes · 1 tsp salt · ½ pt water

Take half a pint of tepid water and cream the yeast in it. Add the warm mashed potatoes, four ounces of flour, and one ounce sugar, mixing till smooth. Cover with a cloth. Leave to rise in a warm place for thirty minutes. Mix again, adding the rest of the sugar and four more ounces of flour. when smooth, add the beaten eggs and the butter, melted but only just warm, also the raisins, salt and the rest of the flour. Mix to a soft dough, knead for five minutes and place in a greased bowl. Cover again and leave for an hour, then divide in two pieces to fit greased tins, cover and leave in warmth until it has doubled its size; about thirty minutes. Bake in the oven for fifty minutes to one hour at 350°F. to 400°F. When it is ready, a test skewer should come out clean.

ciste úill
apple cake

8 oz flour · 3 large cooking apples · 3 oz margarine · 1 egg
2 oz brown sugar · 1 tsp baking powder

Sieve the flour and baking powder together, then rub in the
margarine [or other fat]. Add the sugar, the beaten egg
and the chopped apples, and mix together. If it seems too
dry, add a little milk, but avoid making it too wet. Before
putting it in the oven, sprinkle some sugar on top, then
bake thirty minutes at 400°F.

bonnogai blathach
buttermilk scones

8 oz flour · 2 oz fat · ¼ tsp bread soda · ¼ tsp salt · ¼ pint buttermilk

❖

Sieve the flour, salt and bread soda into a bowl, mixing well, then rub in the fat [margarine, cooking fat, etc.] Add enough buttermilk to make a loose dough. Place on a floured board and knead lightly. Use the palm of the hand to flatten it out into a circle half an inch thick. Cut with two crosses to divide it into eight. Put on a greased baking tin. Bake in a hot oven, 425° F., for fifteen to twenty minutes.

56

pancóga
chille mhantáin
wicklow pancake

4 eggs · 2 cups white breadcrumbs · 1 pint milk · 1 oz
butter · chopped scallions · parsley · thyme · salt · pepper

Beat the eggs, then add the milk, breadcrumbs, scallions
and herbs. Season to taste. Melt the butter and pour
over the mixture. Allow to set over a low heat, and
when firm enough, turn over and cook on the other side.

arán bhocstaí
boxty bread

'b flour · 1 lb cooked and mashed potatoes · 1 lb of raw potatoes · 4 oz melted butter · salt · pepper

Wash and peel one pound of potatoes. Grate into a clean cloth, and wring tightly over a bowl to extract the juice. Place the grated potatoes in a bowl with the mashed potatoes. Allow time for the starch to settle to the bottom of the potato juice, then pour off the liquid. Put the starch in with the potatoes and sieve over the flour, salt and pepper, mixing all thoroughly. Add the melted butter [or bacon fat may be used instead], knead well, and roll out on a floured board. Make into flat round cakes, and mark a cross on top, to make it easy to break in quarters when baked. Put on a greased baking sheet and bake for about forty minutes in the oven at 300°F. Serve hot, split in two with plenty of butter.

bonnóg arain choirc agus bláthaigh
buttermilk oaten bread

9 oz flour · 7 oz fine oatmeal · ½ pint buttermilk · ½ tsp bread soda · ½ tsp salt

Steep the oatmeal overnight in the buttermilk [or sour milk]. Mix together the flour, salt and soda, then stir in the oatmeal. If necessary, a little more milk may be added to keep the dough soft. Knead on a floured board until smooth, then roll out about two inches thick. Cut into four, and bake in a moderate oven for about twentyfive minutes.

bruitin choirce
pratie oaten

1 lb potatoes · 8 oz fine oatmeal · 4 oz butter · salt

Peel, boil and mash the potatoes. While still warm, work in
sufficient fine oatmeal to form a rather soft dough,
adding salt, and enough melted butter to bind it. If
preferred, bacon fat may be substituted. Sprinkle a
generous dusting of oatmeal on a baking board and roll
out the dough quarter to half an inch thick. Cut into
triangles and cook on a greased griddle in a hot oven for
fifteen to twenty minutes. Alternatively, brown both
sides in a frying pan.

pancóga bocstaith
boxty pancakes

½ lb flour · ½ lb cooked & mashed potatoes · ½ lb raw pot
2 oz melted butter · ½ tsp bicarbonate of soda · milk · pep
salt

❧

These are the same ingredients as for boxty bread, with the
addition of soda and milk. Prepare in the same way,
but add bicarbonate of soda and sufficient milk to make
a batter of dropping consistency. Heat a greased pan
and cook spoonfuls of the mixture over a moderate heat.
Turn over to cook both sides evenly. Serve with butter,
and for the sweet-toothed, sprinkle with sugar.

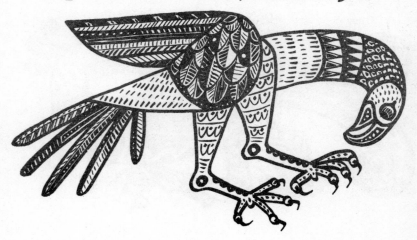

Ciste
bhaile átha cliath
dublin cake

flour · 8 oz butter · 8 oz brown sugar · 8 oz sultanas ·
raisins · 8 oz currants · 4 oz mixed peel · 1 tsp spice ·
4 eggs · 1 tsp baking soda · ½ tsp salt

ream together butter and sugar. Add the eggs one at a time
with a teaspoon of flour. Beat well between each egg. Sift
the flour with the salt, soda and spice. Fold into the
egg mixture. Moisten with a little stout, and stir in
the fruit and mixed peel. Put in a greased tin lined
with greased paper. Bake at 350°F. for three hours,
reducing heat for the last hour.

aran donn
brown bread

1 lb coarse wheat meal · ½ lb white flour · ¾ pint sour
2 tsp salt · 2 tsp baking soda

✤

Mix the wheat meal flour with the white flour, adding salt
and soda. Make a well in the centre and pour in the
milk, mixing with a wooden spoon. Knead dough into a
ball with floured hands. Turn on to a floured board, and
flatten by hand into a circle about one and a half inches
thick. Take a floured knife and mark a cross on top, so
that it is easily broken in quarters when baked. Bake
for twentyfive minutes at 425°F., then reduce heat to
350°F. and allow fifteen more minutes. This bread
should not be cut until six hours after it is taken from the
oven.

✳ Instead of the sour milk, buttermilk or fresh milk can
be used.

Cistí preataí
potato cakes

½ cooked potatoes · 2 oz flour · ½ oz butter · ¼ tsp salt ·
¼ tsp baking powder · milk

Put the sieved flour, salt and baking powder into a bowl,
mixing well, then add the sieved potatoes and the melted
butter. Mix to a smooth dough, adding a little milk if
required. Place on a floured board, kneading until
smooth, and divide in two. Roll out each piece on the
board into a circle about a quarter of an inch thick, then
cut into six or eight triangles. Cook on a hot greased
griddle until nicely brown on both sides. Note: bacon
fat or margarine may be used as the fat.

glóthach maothá
haw jelly

2 lbs haws · 2 lbs apples · 1 tsp ground ginger · 1 tsp g.
cloves · 1 pint water · 1 lb sugar to each pint of juice—

Pick sufficient ripe haws. Wash and dry the apples, and cut
up small. Crab apples may be used if available. Place
all in a pan with the water and cloves. Stir until it
comes to the boil and boil until soft, then strain through
a jelly bag. Add one pound of sugar for each pint of
juice. Stir until the sugar melts. Bring to the boil and
boil quickly until it sets when tested. Pour into jars.

peirsil glothach
parsley jelly

1 lb sugar to each pint of juice · parsley · water · lemon rind

Wash and drain the parsley. Fully grown parsley should
be used. Put into a lined saucepan, pressing down well,
and cover with cold water. Heat slowly, and then boil
for half an hour. Strain through a jelly bag, re-straining
if it is not clear. Allow one pound of sugar for each
pint of liquid. Boil the liquid for five minutes, then
add the warm sugar and boil until it sets when tested.
When lemon flavouring is wanted, tie the rind parings
in a muslin bag and add to the jelly for the last few
minutes of boiling. Pour into small jars.

cíor mheala·
buíocháin uhilis
honeycomb·'yellow man'

12 oz sugar· 2 oz butter· 4 tblsp golden syrup· 1 tblsp
water· 1 tsp vinegar· 2 tsp of baking soda

Melt the butter in a heavy pan, and add the sugar, syrup
and water. Stir over a low heat until a little of the
mixture makes a firm ball when dropped into cold water.
Remove from the heat and mix in the vinegar. Now add
the baking soda, stirring rapidly as the mixture froths
up, and quickly pour into an oiled tin. Break up into
small pieces when cold. This confection does not keep well,
and is best eaten fairly soon.

GRUTH AGUS MEADHG
buttermilk curd

1 gallon buttermilk · fresh raspberries or strawberries ·
sugar

♣

Place the freshly churned buttermilk in a double muslin bag or a linen jelly bag, and suspend over a crock to drain. Leave until there is a fairly dry curd. Mix the fruit with the sweetened curd, and serve with double cream. If preferred, the fruit and curd may be served in separate dishes. In olden times, Irish monks were allowed to drink the whey [drained off the curd] when they had a day of fasting.

beoir sinséir
ginger beer

1 oz root ginger · 1 lb sugar · 1 oz yeast · 1 oz cream of tartar · 1 lemon

Place the bruised ginger in a bowl, adding the sugar, cream of tartar, and lemon rind and juice. Pour on a gallon of boiling water and stir thoroughly with a wooden spoon. When lukewarm, mix the yeast in a little water with a teaspoon of sugar, and when it begins to froth, stir in with the rest. Leave for one day, after which it can be filled into screw top bottles.

caiṗe gaelach
iṙish coṗṗee

1 double measure Irish whiskey · 1 cup strong, hot, black coffee · 1 tblsp double cream · 1 heaped tsp sugar

❖

Warm a stemmed whiskey glass. Put in the sugar and add enough very hot coffee to dissolve it, and stir well. Top up with Irish whiskey to within one inch of the brim. Hold a teaspoon across the glass, curved side up, and pour the cold cream carefully over it, slowly, so that it floats on the surface of the coffee. The cream is not to be stirred in; the hot beverage is drunk THROUGH it.

puins bheath-uisge
irish whiskey punch

1 measure Irish whiskey · 1½ tsp brown sugar · cloves
sliced lemon

✤

heat a glass goblet, put in the brown sugar with enough boiling water to dissolve it. Add the whiskey, cloves and sliced lemon, and top up with more boiling water. This is a traditional Irish nightcap. The word "whiskey" comes from the Irish Gaelic, UISGEBEATHA, pronounced "wishkebaha."

Conversion Table

The following are approximate conversions from the British Imperial system to U.S and metric measurements.

BRITISH IMPERIAL	U·S	METRIC
1 ounce	1 ounce	28 grams
1 pound [16 ounces]	1 pound [16 ounces]	454 grams
1 pint [20 fluid ounces]	1¼ pints [U:S pint=16 fl.oz]	568 ml
1 quart [40 fluid ounces]	1¼ quarts	1136 ml

Note that in the British Imperial system —

    1 teaspoon equals 5ml
    2 teaspoons equal 1 dessertspoon
    3 teaspoons equal 1 tablespoon

Standard spoon sizes are slightly smaller in the American system and therefore all spoon measures should be taken generously in the U.S. & Canada.

❖

weights and Measures

The Imperial system of weights and measures has been used throughout this book. Cooks in North America should remember that the Imperial pint consists of 20 fluid ounces and is thus larger than the American pint of 16 fluid ounces. Standard spoon sizes are also smaller in the American system and therefore all spoon measures shou be taken generously in America.

∴ METRIC CONVERSION ∴

	weights			liquids	
1 ounce	equals	28 grams	1 teaspoon	equals	5 ml
2 ounces	"	56 grams	1 dessertspoon	"	10 ml
3 ounces	"	85 grams	1 tablespoon	"	15 ml
4 ounces	"	113 grams	¼ pint	"	142 ml
5 ounces	"	227 grams	½ pint	"	284 ml
16 ounces [1 lb]	"	454 grams	1 pint	"	568 ml

index

Meat

Sweets

Drinks